BOBBIE HARRIS

The Journey for Proofreading Skills

First edition

This book was professionally typeset on Reedsy.
Find out more at reedsy.com

Contents

1

Introduction

Welcome to the informational book about Proofreading Skills. My name is Bobbie Harris and I am excited to give you a viewpoint from a layman's perspective. I am not a professional proofreader and occasionally do proofread for a few of my friends and my family, and have had the opportunity to research the topic. I am excited about the information in this book as it compiles the basic skills and understanding that are needed for proofreading with a different perspective. This is not a comprehensive guide, but a generalization of some of the things I have learned.

A brief background about myself. . . I have had numerous opportunities to learn Grammar, Spelling, and punctuation. I have always been able to spot mistakes, not only in writing, but in everyday life, and in films that the editors miss. I have worked in the Clerical industry since I was 15 years old, (many years believe me), either in accounting, customer service, Notary Public situations, and other opportunities to learn writing and proofreading different documents. I currently write my own books and still to this day cringe when I see a mistake or hear someone use the wrong pronoun or verb tense. (I learned a long time ago not to correct people as they do get defensive.) Enough about me, Let's talk about the reason you picked this book to read and see if I can give you an insight into what the skills are for a proofreader.

2

CAN YOU DO PROOFREADING

Proofreading is not for everyone, but if you have the skills and the ability to read over documents for Grammatical, Punctuation, Spelling, and Capitalization errors then you may be able to be a proofreader. You don't have to memorize the rules for proofreading, but you do have to have a general grasp of the basics and the willingness to research if you are not sure of what a particular rule is. This includes knowing the basis for these skills and keeping up to date with the latest new slangs and idioms that would go with the skills. I for one have always thought that the word "Learnt" was not used and should be spelled learned. While doing research I found that the word is now used in the past present tense, but still to my ears I still hear learnt as a word was not acceptable, it sounds strange. This is why research and an open mind will aid you tremendously in being a proofreader.

The competition for a job is fierce and you do have to take a proofreading test to qualify for a paying job with any of the companies that you would like to work with. I have taken a few of these tests and you need to remember for the test you need to make sure there are no distractions for the duration. Most of the companies before the test will have instructions and how long the test should take, once again I stress you have to make sure you are not interrupted during the test. I did take a test with a major company (No Names) and one of my Dogs actually was hurt during the test. I did not have enough time to complete the test, but was able to contact the company and they actually were able to give me a second chance. Just so you know this was a special circumstance and most companies will not give you a second chance as they post the rules and instructions before you take the test. Of course you can start your own business involving a whole set of skills including being a sales person for your skills and what you are able to do.

There are numerous classes and videos you can engage in to write that will do spell check and punctuation for you while you are writing. These are what I call a guide as they do not replace the human factor for the flow of the document and the research. It takes the ability to be able to find the errors on a consistent and daily basis for hours on end that a full time job requires. You have to be willing to learn if you plan on working in the field, because face it we as humans do not know everything, and the English and other languages are ever evolving. I encourage anyone who is looking to get into this field to research it thoroughly as the programs we use do not take into account the dialogs of regions. I will try to include the basic information for proofreading and touch on some of the ones I was not aware of when I started this journey.

3

THE SKILLS OF PROOFREADING

One of the first skills you will have to possess or learn on your journey is Adeptness. This is one of the main skills as it does take some tenacity and grit to make sure you are at the top of your game for the industry. If you have the desire to put in the effort to stay with-it to do the research and have a genuine ability to work on your skills you could be successful in this field. You also need to be able to have a very open mind as some things can be hard to grasp and understand.

Your attitude is paramount in becoming a Proofreader as you not only work alone, and the hours are not usually 9 to 5, but you have to be flexible with your hours. If you are not the kind of person that can sit for long hours reading, then you would not have the attitude for the career. Proofreading tends to not be fast-paced, but you do have to be able to get a project finished and

back to the client, or next in line to edit, in a timely manner. You have to be able to work with authors to make sure you do not change the idea they are trying to convey and the style they are using to write. Every author I have read or done Proofreading for has a certain style, because each person has a different outlook on life from different experiences. That is why you see so many different books on one topic, because each perspective is different. Your attitude will make a difference in everything you do as a Proofreader because it gives you the drive to learn more, to have the desire to be excellent, the persistence to keep going when you encounter roadblocks. It also gives you the ability to understand that sometimes you have to work outside your comfort zone and not get stuck in a rut about what you can accomplish. (More in depth later)

There are numerous opportunities since the dawn of the typewriter and internet programs that seem to do everything for you be it grammar, punctuation checks, spell check, typesetting, and graphics for you to use. These still do not detour a determined proofreader from learning more ways to capitalize on the advantages and drawbacks but to be more valuable to the prospective client or company.

You also need to know what proofreading is not. The proofreader does not do rewriting or do major editing. They do not check historical values or verify research. They do not do formatting. They are not copy writers or production managers or typists. It will be a good idea to know what each of these roles do so that you can be a better proofreader. (We will touch on this subject later.)

So is Proofreading for you? Can you see yourself on a day to day basis reading any kind of document and finding the mistakes or do they just jump out at you like they do for me, then you probably have the skill set for the job. You may have to hone your skills and do some research, but that is part of learning and becoming the best you can be for you.

4

The Stages

The proofreader is involved in all stages of the printed process, whether it is on paper copy or electronic copy. Some of these stages are not all required as this is just a general list and not for every scenario.

Stage one: Starts the process with the writing of the copy and then will usually go to an Editor and then to the typist or the editor to make the changes in the document.

Stage two: The copy then goes to a designer for the typeset and they will pass it on to a typesetter, who will set the type and make a reader's proof and will check for errors. The copy then will go back to the designer as they will check for typeset and layout correction. The proofreader will then check for errors, consistency issues, and checks to make sure the typeset was followed correctly.

Stage 3: The typesetter will make any changes and send back a revised copy and then is reviewed by the proofreader again (making it available for the editor, designer, typesetter, writer, and perhaps others). This is repeated until all proofs are accurate and approved by all parties involved.

Stage 4: The production manager sends the proof to the printer and the copy is printed. This has a final step that all the departments including the proofreader make a final check before it is printed.

Stage 5: The copy is then printed.

As a professional proofreader you will have numerous opportunities for different types of jobs in the industry and different levels you can achieve as well as broadening your horizons to one of the other jobs. Just make sure you understand the job that is being offered and what is required by you.

5

THE LEVELS

Beginner: This is entry level Proofreading and is where the majority of people will start, unless you have extensive job experience. This level only catches the most basic of proofreading from the original document by correcting misspellings, incorrect math, incorrect word breaks, typing errors, and format style.

Intermediate I: This level includes the Beginner level and is responsible for grammatical and punctuation errors, and is the next step for the professional to achieve.

Intermediate II: This level includes the previous two levels and is skilled in typeface identification and type specification. These are learned skills and are not something that needs to be memorized as you can look up a typeface if you or the program you are using does not identify it.

Intermediate III: The level is inclusive with the first three levels and also has the advanced knowledge of language and type. These skills are changing from time to time so you would need to do research and learning to make sure you have the latest information.

Senior: This level of course is the highest in the Proofreading skills. It does include the first 4 and a knowledge of some copywriting skills. I will not go into copywriting as it is not the focus of my book.

You will also have to be familiar with two ways to proofread, and is determined by a factor of things, such as is it the first time you have proofread the copy or is it a printed copy or a computer screen.

Comparison reading

There are several ways for comparison reading and it is just what it sounds like. It is comparing a live copy with the dead copy. You will also watch for bad word breaks, type mistakes, and misspellings, but at this time you do not make those corrections,

Reading alone: You will compare the (old copy) now referred to as the (dead copy) and the (new copy) now referred to as the (Live copy). It does depend on which stage of the process you are in as to what is required for your job. Essentially you could have several drafts that you will have to proofread before it goes to print.

Reading with another person: The copyholder will read the dead copy word for word including punctuation and format while you check the live copy. Watching for the same things you would have if reading alone.This method will give you a different perspective on the copy.

Using a tape recorder: You can use this if you do not have a copyholder. Read the dead copy to a tape recorder making sure you read slowly, stating each syllable and punctuation and every thing that a copyholder would read. Play the recording back and compare it to the live copy.

Non-comparison (Dry or silent) reading

There are instances when you will not have a dead copy to compare with a live copy, this is called non-comparison reading. It is sometimes helpful at this stage to read your copy aloud, making a different circumstance for you to pick up mistakes.

If you do use a copyholder it would be to your advantage to learn or at least have a knowledge of the Copyholders Vocabulary.

6

THE RIGHT ATTITUDE FOR SUCCESS

THE RIGHT ATTITUDE FOR SUCCESS
I would not feel I have added enough instructions if I did not go back to Attitude. As a proofreader you are responsible for doing the incredible. You have to find mistakes that others have missed and make sure you have not missed any in the process, making the job stressful.

We will now look at some of the ways you can choose to help with the stress.

Clear the room makes it easier to concentrate without any social distractions. You can also let others know you will be busy for a certain amount of time.

Fatigue is detrimental to proofreading as you need to maintain focus. If you have a long document you would want to take frequent breaks or work in segments.

Boredom is almost inevitable if you are even a "seasoned proofreader". It could be a number of things, but to counteract boredom you could make a game of it. For instance see how many mistakes you can find in a chapter and then go back over it and count to see if you have found more mistakes. This will give you something to work towards and also help you focus.

Reading the directions is paramount to make sure you know what is expected from you and there could be answers to any question you may have. If you need clarification on something make sure you reach out to the person you need to.

Methodically read with comparison reading first if possible word for word at least once for each stage, typed manuscript, typed galleys, and printer's proof. Read as many times as you need to to create your style sheet and then reread until there is no dead text to compare. Then read the copy aloud until you are sure there are no other errors.

Read slowly at a comfortable pace and if you do not have the time it would be wise to come back to it.

Reading with a rhythm not only will help you catch mistakes for different types of documents. You can look from letter to letter and it is useful if you have a very small or large type, and foreign languages. You can read word for word or you can read two to three words at a time.

Look out for the red flags or warning signals to take a second look at the work. This could be certain things you recognize as excessive punctuation to long or short sentences.

7

STYLE SHEETS

STYLE SHEETS AND THEIR USE

A style sheet is not just a random set of instructions for the Proofreader, but is a guide used to convey the mistakes that need changing and any questions you may have for the next level person to make changes. There are different style sheets for each style of copy you will encounter and if you work for a company they may have already adopted or made their own style sheet for you to use.

Some of the points of style you may be working with (not a complete list) are as follows.

Format

Spelling and Capitalization

Hyphenations

Numerals

Plurals, positives and punctuation

Abbreviations

Special treatment

Dates

Foreign words

Facts

Trademarks and service marks, copyright marks, and logotypes
Footnotes, bibliographies, tables, and charts
Miscellaneous

These are important and I will lightly touch on each one.

Format

Format is the (layout) or physical appearance of the copy. This includes the typeset, size of margins, other characteristics that include the copy.

Spelling and capitalization

You need to include in your stylesheet the proper nouns and the proper spelling and capitalization for names such as N.S.A. Company. This could be misspelled later on in the document and if you made a note on your stylesheet you do not have to check back in the document later. Remember that words can be spelled differently and it is a good idea to check with the resources you have to verify which spelling would be preferred by that source.

Hyphenations

Words that are hyphenated may cause a problem either later on in the copy or due to style or what is needed for attractiveness. List these on your stylesheet and any words that could be hyphenated later in the copy.

Numerals

Numbers are more complex due to the writing style of the author or what the editor thinks would look best for that copy. A preferred method is to spell out the numbers from one to ninety-nine and use numbers for 100 and above. Make sure you note on your stylesheet what is being used in the document so it can be consistent throughout the copy.

Plurals, possessives, and punctuation

Each of these have rules you should be familiar with and if you do not have a good grasp of these rules there are numerous books and articles for you to reference. Plurals and possessives have rules that you need to be familiar with but they can be influenced by style. There is no punctuation style and copy is either correct or wrong. Your job is to make sure the punctuation is correct by the rules. Note on your stylesheet the changes so you can check thru the copy for consistency.

Abbreviations

It is important that you grasp a few things about abbreviations. Not all are treated with consistency throughout the copy, causing a problem for the Proofreader. You will need to notate on your stylesheet what is being used and also to check your reference dictionary to make sure it is correct. Some abbreviations are not acceptable, one such example is 'til for the word until, most of the experts (but not all) will agree that the acceptable word is till. The word thru is not an acceptable abbreviation for through. Check with your resources.

Special treatment

If the writer or editor believes that a misspelled word justifies the means for the copy it is a good idea to make sure it is on your stylesheet so you can reference it later. This could also be handy if you are proofreading with the same author or editor. Make sure you are making sure this is the normal or all the copy you will be proofreading.

Dates

Dates have many different styles and there are a few rules to follow. If a comma precedes the year then a comma should follow the year unless it is at the end of a sentence. Make sure you note the particular style for the copy you are proofreading and make on your stylesheet. This will make it easier to check consistency throughout the copy.

Foreign Words

The written copy in English may contain some foreign words and should be included in your stylesheet, making sure you put the accent marks where they are placed. All foreign words should be *italicized*, or underlined unless it has been adopted by Americans.

Facts

As the proofreader you are not responsible for the factual information or inconsistencies you find in the document. Instead, note in your stylesheet any inconsistencies that you may notice like "There were 3 deer standing on the side of the road" and later when this was mentioned again it happened to be 5 deer.

Trademarks and Service Marks

If you are working with non-fictional copy you may encounter trademarks (™), and service marks (sm), and registration marks (®) make sure you list them in your stylesheet and these cannot be deviated from as these are common laws governing the use of each. You need to know these laws. Service marks and trademarks are included in the "Trademark Act of 1946".

The marks are used to identify the owner of the register name and is common to add a footnote or at the end of the copy with the owner's information for the mark.

Copyright marks

Some foreign countries do not accept anything but the copyright marks so it is important to have those referenced at the end of the copy. This is another way to protect the rights of the original author. Make sure you check the copy to make sure the copyright is used correctly and the dates and names are correct.

Logo types

Corporate logos are used to create a visual image of the corporation. These are often registered with the U.S. Patent and Trademark office. It is essential that you nitrate these on your stylesheet for later reference in the copy.

Footnotes, Bibliographies, Tables, and Charts

The style set in the copy will be what you will notate on your stylesheet just to make sure it is consistent throughout the copy.

Miscellaneous

You may use this section for anything you have not included in the previous sections.

Seeing what is involved in a stylesheet makes it easier for you to be familiar with them as you progress in your endeavor to be the best proofreader you can be. The stylesheet needs to be updated and distributed to all parties that are involved in the copy.

8

UNDERSTANDING THE WRITERS STYLE

UNDERSTANDING THE WRITER'S STYLE

Study It

Make sure you check your resources for misused words and your best resource is a good dictionary. You can also make note of words you may not understand or have heard as the languages are bound to change. Always contact the editor or author for any clarification concerning a particular word. I have found words I didn't even know existed until they were on a written page that I was proofreading. I had to ask the author exactly what they meant and still looked it up in the dictionary for my own knowledge.

Spell it right

Spelling can be tedious and for some people down right hard. Making it necessary for a Proofreading career. Incorrect word usage is something to make note of and keep in mind for consistency in the copy. If it is misused in one sentence it could happen later in the document. If you are not sure of a spelling look it up in a dictionary the way it is spelled and if you can't find it look as it is pronounced. Make sure you read the full definition as words sometimes and have several meanings.

Foreign words

If you do not know the language or are not fluent the meaning can be elusive to you. If this is the case then you only look for typographical errors.

Know Mechanics

You will find that not all, or at least most, writers have just a basic knowledge of the mechanics for grammar and punctuation. You may be the only recourse to make sure the copy is corrected and understood correctly. There are numerous books and articles on the mechanics so make sure you brush up on them from time to time to keep you current.

When to Query

We all sometimes second guess ourselves, but do not be afraid to ask questions. This could mean the difference in conveying the correct idea to the reader.

9

PROOFREADERS MARKS AND TOOLS

PROOFREADERS MARKS

Proofreader marks are vital communication resources for any copy and the team you may be working with. These you do need to be familiar with. There are references in books or online articles that will give you the marks and what they mean. I will not include these in my book as the list is easy to obtain.

When you are using a proofreaders mark you will place in the text and a corresponding explanation in the documents margin. Make sure you make the use the right margin for the right column and the left margin for the left column. If only one column uses the same one consistently. Don't invent new proof marks; this will only confuse anyone on your team.

TYPEFACE

Typeface is still in use even with the constant use of computers and programs to set the Type. There are one-hundred thousand or more fonts to choose from and more being made up each day. Every proofreader should know what makes one font different from another. This area is very broad but you do need to at least look into this area so you will have a working knowledge of the different typeset as it could be very valuable in certain jobs.

TYPESETTERS LANGUAGE

Typesetters have type specifications or (specs) or makeup, and are written in a very simple technical language. You should be familiar with these specs as you will have to follow the directions when written. The typesetter has three primary pieces of information they have to use.

The type font

The point size of the type and the leading

Copy Depth, usually in Picas, and margins and other justifications.

THE PROOFREADERS TOOLS

Two 6-inch non transparent rulers Dictionary

Magnifying glass Grammar/punctuation handbook

Fine-line, indelible-ink red pen Word usage reference

Lead pencil (colored) Stylebook and/or Style Sheet

Pica and point gauges Key to proofreaders marks

World Atlas

Foreign Language Dictionaries, as required

Trade names reference

Typeface guide

Graphic Arts handbook

These are the tools of the trade and you may pick up more as you progress or strive to learn more.

10

OTHER JOBS IN THE FIELD

OTHER JOBS IN THE FIELD
Once you have mastered or have a good knowledge of the skills you need to be familiar with for proofreading you need to have a grasp of the kind of other areas the copy will be sent to.

First is the writer, They of course write the copy.

The editor will then edit and revise the copy.

The designer will do the typesetting if it is available

The typist if it has not been done previously will retype the copy.

The production manager will send the copy to the editor when it has been proofread and Approved.

The printer will complete a first draft of the copy and then will be sent back to the production manager and the copy may go through the process again to make sure all mistakes have been fixed. The proofreader has a hand in every stage and copy may come back to you several times.

JOB OPPORTUNITIES

There are many job opportunities to have a self made business. One is a partner that will write for you to keep them on track. To set this up you advertise to proofread say 1500 words per day (or the amount the writer agrees to), this gives you a steady job for several weeks to months with one client and you can set up several such jobs. This kills two birds with one stone as it will also help the writer to make sure they get the copy done on time and you have to get it back to them in a timely manner.

Be a co-author, of course most proofreaders will tell you they do not do co-author, but if you are the only person to critique the copy and you make the changes yourself then you are already doing this job.

Selling is part of making your business work. Not in the way that you would sell books or even miscellaneous items. You are selling yourself to the general public and the authors of the books, magazines, and other periodicals that may come your way. The more you know about your benefits and the proofreading you have already accomplished.

HOW TO FIND A CLIENT

You may try to go to a Facebook writing group to get your clients, but I would discourage this as most of the writers are looking for a one time hand out for their copy. I would start in a bloggers forum as the work is rewarding, fast paced, and can be a daily job for your proofreading experience. The bloggers will also more readily post a review for you to use as you progress and to help with your client list. To start you can offer discounts for/or upto certain pages to get more clients.

REFERRALS

While you are building your business, ask permission from the clients you are proofreading for, to use their publications as a reference. Later when you are ready to set up a web page for your business you will already have permission and the client could be asked to write a short testimonial about your services on your website.

11

CONCLUSION

CONCLUSION
There is a lot of material to go over in this book and by no means is it inclusive. I did not add all of the tools and information you will need to succeed in being a great Proofreader. There are many opportunities in the field of Proofreading from working for a major company, or doing one on one with an author or even owning and managing your own business. Thank you for the opportunity to help expand your knowledge. I hope you have found my book interesting and informative. Please leave a review on Amazon

12

RESOURCES

Resources:

The Journey for Proofreading skills (Proofreading Secrets of Best-Selling Authors ed.). (2016). Kathy Ide.

Anderson, L. (2006b). *McGraw-Hill's Proofreading Handbook* (2nd ed.). McGraw Hill.

The Pocket Book of Proofreading: A guide to freelance proofreading & copy-editing. (2014). William Critchley.

A Proofreading Companion: Tips, Tools & Strategies for the Professional Proofreader. (2019). Jennifer Karchmer.

How to Start a Successful Proofreading Business: Catch the New Wave in the Kindle Revolution (Gary Thaller ed.). (n.d.). Gary Thaller.